Contents

Why a book of phonic games?

Listening to people talking is an essential part of learning to talk. Spoken language breaks down into sentences, phrases, words and individual sounds (phonemes). Phonics is the building block on which all spoken and written language is based. Children learn to listen to and break down the talking that they hear from a very early age. As adults we tend to think about 'letters' when we consider how a word is made up. However, long before they know anything about letters, children are dealing with sounds (phonemes).

This book is all about sounds in words. I hope you will find it a fun, useful way of helping your child to develop their skills with phonics. In doing so you will be supporting their speech sounds, their spoken and written language and their spelling. All of these skills rely on effective phonic abilities.

What is phonics?

Phonics is about the individual sounds which make up a spoken word. Every word is made up of individual phonemes. A phoneme is a unit of sound that, if it changes, would change the meaning of the word. So, for example, the word 'hat' is made of three phonemes *h*, *a* and *t*. If the *t* phoneme is changed to an *m* phoneme this changes the word to 'ham' and the meaning is changed. If the *a* phoneme is changed to *i* the word changes again, to 'him', and again the meaning is changed. There are some phonemes which require more than one letter when written down. Here are some examples: *sh*, *ch*, *th*. These are single units of sound.

Letter sounds versus letter names

When you see the letter *b*, what do you say: *buh* or *bee*? The first gives the letter its letter sound. Saying the letter sound is sometimes referred to as the phonic alphabet. The second, *bee*, gives it its letter name.

The table over the page will help you with the differences between the letter sound and letter name pronunciations.

Letter sound	Written letter	How to pronounce the letter name
a	a	ay
buh	b	bee
cuh	c	see
duh	d	dee
eh	e	ee
fuh	f	eff
guh	g	gee
huh	h	aitch
i	i	eye
juh	j	jay
kuh	k	kay
luh	l	ell
muh	m	em
nuh	n	en
o	o	oh
puh	p	pee
quh	q	queue
ruh	r	are
suh	s	ess
tuh	t	tee
uh	u	you
vuh	v	vee
wuh	w	double you
x	x	ex
yuh	y	why
zuh	z	zed

How phonics affects speech and language development

Children learn to talk by listening to the language being spoken around them. They hear words and learn to recognise them because they have heard them many times. How do they recognise them? Through identifying and storing in their memories the sounds (phonemes) in the word. When they want to say the word, they recall the sounds they have stored and have a go at saying the word. Children with poor phonic abilities are likely to have more difficulties in learning to talk and in understanding and using new words, as well as problems in pronouncing the words correctly.

How phonics affects reading and writing

Children often learn to read by recognising whole words and saying the word shape that they see. This requires good visual memory. However, as the child progresses they will also need to be able to look at a series of letters and work out how to put those letters together to make a word. This requires effective phonic skills: being able to translate the written letters into sounds and then blend them to make a word. For example, a-n-i-m-a-l when blended makes the word 'animal'.

Most children will spell a word by saying it out loud, trying to identify the individual sounds and writing them down. This is also a phonic skill: hearing the separate sounds within a word. Children with speech sound problems will often spell as they speak. For example, a child may say fum for 'thumb', and spell it 'fum' as those are the sounds they hear when they say it. Children who struggle with breaking the word down in to syllables and then into phonemes will find it hard to spell a word, unless they have remembered how to spell it or use a good visual memory (asking themselves 'Does this word look right?').

Having fun with syllables

The games

The games are presented in sections according to where you might play them. Within each section you will find there are syllable games, games for individual sounds within words and rhyming games. The syllable games will be much easier than the other sets of games and you are advised to start with some of these.

Introduction to syllable games

Syllables are great fun. We march to them, beat out a rhythm to them and clap them without even thinking about them. When it comes to listening to the sounds that we use for speech, syllables are the place to start. Words split first into syllables and then into individual sounds.

Take the long word 'caterpillar'. It has a lot of different sounds in it, and as a new word it may be overwhelming for anyone to listen to and have a go at saying. However, once you break it down into syllables, each part is manageable:

cat-er-pill-ar

Think about how you would learn to say a new word. You would break it down into manageable chunks, listen to the sounds in each chunk and then have a go at saying it.

Children who need extra help with phonics will benefit from playing games with syllables; this tunes them in to paying attention to the sounds in words and prepares them for tackling the much harder skill of identifying the individual sounds that make up a word.

The syllable games in this book are designed to be fun. Work out the syllable numbers together by clapping, jumping, stamping and beating out (as directed in the instructions). Always say and clap, stamp, and so on, unless directed otherwise in the game. The games are not for you to test your child's ability, but to give them extra practice of a skill. Sometimes hold back, and see if your child can do the task without your help, then join in and do it together. Always take your turn in the games. Do not make comments about their getting it wrong; rather encourage another go with you helping out. They will learn through success and positive feedback.

A word of warning: Playing games with syllables requires you to say the word the way you normally would, and not distort the saying of it. If you change the way you are saying the word to help them hear the syllables, your child may think that is how it should be said. For instance, you may think it would be helpful to emphasise the last sound of a word so your child can hear it clearly, but this may result in changing the number of syllables.

Here are some common mistakes:

- sch-ool (when you want them to hear the sc sound) will become two syllables when it is only one;
- ca-t will end up sounding like *ca-tuh* if you overemphasise the last sound, and will make it two syllables when it is one;
- computer has three syllables, but only the second syllable, *pu*, is stressed or emphasised. The *com* and *er* syllables are a little less emphasised. You need to try to keep that pattern when saying the word, otherwise it turns into robot-type speech.

Introduction to games for individual sounds

Once your child can break a word down into the number of syllables, the next step is to separate the first sound from the rest of the syllable. For example, sh-ell, m-ilk, tr-ee. These games are designed to help your child practise this skill. It is very important at this stage that you use the letter sounds when working out the first sounds in words; avoid the letter names. (See the table of letter sounds on p. 6.)

As with the syllable games, if your child is struggling then join in with them and help them out. Give them lots of examples of what you are trying to do. If the game becomes one in which they provide you with the item and you do the working out, that is fine for a time as they will be learning from hearing you identify the sounds.

You will see that there are some games where the object is to identify the last sound of a word. Think carefully about these and note that the focus is the final sound, not the final letter. So, for example, the last sound in 'flower' is *uh*, and the last sound in 'ice' is *s*. That is the response you need from your child at that point. If your child is reading and spelling you can use this opportunity to draw out the differences between what we say and what we write. If they tell you that the last sound in 'ice' is *e*, an appropriate response would be, 'That is the last letter, well done! Can you tell me the last sound? What sound can you hear?'

When playing games with final sounds, you need to be careful not to distort the pronunciation of the word by overemphasising the last sound or syllable of the word. For example, 'bird' is different from *birduh*.

Rhyming games

Each section also has a set of games concerned with rhymes. These are designed to help children listen to rhyming pairs and make up words that rhyme. This skill is an advanced one, and shows good phonic abilities. Rhyming involves identifying the first sound, removing it and selecting and then substituting another phoneme to make a real word. So, for example, with 'sun' remove the *s* and substitute the phoneme *sh* to make the new word 'shun'; with 'tap', remove the *t* and replace it with *m* to give the new word 'map'.

Rhyming games can be great fun and children enjoy the silly sounds they make. If your child can generate rhymes but they are not real words ('hat' rhymes with 'lat', 'comb' rhymes with 'pome'), this should be praised; they are showing the skill of rhyme, but are not able yet to know whether the phonemes they select make a real word or not.

How to play the games

You will find that most of the games do not require any equipment or preparation. Those that do should need only things you can find round the house or when you are out and about.

Each game has some ideas for extending the activity a little – making it harder or easier or suggesting some changes to make it even more interesting. It is hoped that this will encourage you to adapt the games for you and your child.

There is a balance of games in which your child has to listen to and work out the sounds, and games in which they have to think of and find things with a particular sound. They will always find it easier to listen to you and then work out the sounds than to work them out for themselves. Start with the ones they find easy and then move on those that will stretch them a little.

Photocopiable resources

At the back of the book you will find some photocopiable materials for you to copy and use, including a page of pictures of things that rhyme. These are intended as a start to your making your own personalised pictures to use with your child. Think about their interests – they may be cars, countries, animals or football teams – and gather pictures that will be really motivating for them. You can draw your own; search for them on the internet; cut them out of papers, catalogues and magazines; or get an older sibling, artistic uncle or grandma to help out. Be careful not to have the written word on your pictures. All these games are concerned with sounds and sometimes the spelling of a word may be confusing.

Finally

The games in this book are designed for you to be able to play with phonics wherever you are: at home, in the car and out and about in general. Each game itself should be fun, and the rules are not important. What is important is that you are providing your child with an opportunity to practise their phonic skills. Remember that these are games, not tests. If your child is struggling or getting things wrong, use that as an opportunity to have a go with them. Always help. Don't leave them to flounder; the games are not about passing and failing, but about practice.

All the games may be played with one child and one adult. They can easily be expanded to include brothers and sisters, friends, grandparents, and so on.

Words are all around us, and therefore so are speech sounds, so go out there and have some fun!

At home

✪ **Syllable games**

Animal Clapping

Breakfast Clapping

Kitchen Drums

Out of the Hat

Pick a Number

Post Boxes

Syllable Lotto

Washing Basket Rap

✪ **First sound games**

Animal Alliteration

Bath-time Fun

Book Worms

Feely Bag

Finger Spelling

Fun at Meal-time

I'm Thinking of ...

Icing Biscuits

Let's go Shopping

Running to Sound

Sounds Collage

Spin and Say

Think and Draw

What's in this Room?

✪ **Last sound games**

Cross it off

Tiddlywinks

Where's the Spinner?

Word Mime

✪ **Rhyming games**

Guess my Picture

Model Animals

Monster Names

Nursery Rhyme Time

Playdough

Rhyming Consequences

Rhyming Hide and Seek

Animal Clapping

 What do I need?

Books with a range of animal pictures

 How to play

Children love cuddling up with you and sharing a book. This activity provides a way of practising syllables as well as sharing time together.

Simply look at the pictures together. As you name the animals, say and clap out the number of syllables.

Ra-bbit
El-e-phant
Dung-beet-le
La-dy-bird

 Some more ideas

What is the most common number of syllables?

What is the longest animal name (in terms of syllables) that you can find?

You don't always need to clap to work out the syllables, but a physical movement will help your child to separate the word into its syllables. There are other ways of doing it. You can try nodding with each syllable, patting your knee, stamping your feet, and so on.

Breakfast Clapping

 What do I need?

Nothing. This game is an extension of your normal breakfast routine.

 How to play

This is a game that demonstrates how you can play with syllables in words wherever you are and whatever you are doing.

The game will help your child listen to and practise working out syllables in everyday words and phrases.

You will have your normal chat about breakfast, but will clap it out as you say it. Each clap will be for one syllable.

Here are some examples:

- Shob-na-what-do-you-want-for-break-fast?
- Mel-vin-come-and-get-your-corn-flakes.
- Do-you-want-hon-ey-or-black-curr-ant-jam?

Try to get your child to reply in the same way. They may need you to help with this at first. It may help to clap their hands in the rhythm of the words to start with.

Make sure you always say the words as you clap, and try to keep to the natural rhythm of the words even though you are separating the syllables.

 Some more ideas

Have some fun trying to find the breakfast item with the most syllables: blackcurrant jam is four syllables; can you beat that?

You don't have to confine yourself to clapping the syllables. You could stamp them, nod you head to them or tap them on the table.

Kitchen Drums

 What do I need?

Pots and pans, some wooden spoons

 How to play

Most children love making lots of noise. This game helps them split words into syllables while having great fun bashing your pots and pans.

Let your child get out a range of pans and containers from your kitchen cupboards. They will also need some wooden spoons (and other beaters if available) for the drum kit.

Have fun listening to the range of noises you can make together. Once this excitement has settled down, you can introduce some rhythms for your child to copy. For example:

_ •• _ ••   or   _ _ •• _ _ ••

Take turns to beat a rhythm and copy it. Then add words to the beats. These may be single words, phrases or sentences, depending on how your child is coping with breaking words down into syllables.

Here are some examples:

- Ke-ttle
- Straw-be-rry-jam
- Dir-ty-plate
- What's-for-lunch?
- The-bu-tter-is-on-the-ta-ble
- The-dish-wash-er-is-near-ly-fin-ished

 Some more ideas

Have a drumming conversation. One asks the question and beats it out; the other answers with words and beats.

For example:

Q: Are-you-hun-gry?
A: Yes-I'm-starv-ing.
Q: What-shall-we-make? Toast-or-sand-wich-es?
A: Tu-na-sand-wich-es-and-tom-a-toes.

Out of the Hat

This is a game of surprises that you can enjoy with all the family.

 What do I need?

A hat (or drawstring bag); everyday items that will fit in it – for example, pen, car, teddy, Lego® brick, glove, pencil sharpener, necklace, calculator, shampoo, curly straw

 How to play

The first time you play, it is probably best for you to put some items in the hat. Ask your child to close their eyes and take an item out of the hat. They may like to guess what it is before they open their eyes. Are they right? Then, together, say what the item is and clap the number of syllables in the word. Continue until all the items have been pulled out.

Next time, let your child fill the hat with things from round the house. You close your eyes, guess and clap the syllables.

 Some more ideas

Can your child tell you how many syllables there are without saying the word out loud?

Take the hat round the house, and each time you play fill it with things from different rooms.

Which item has the largest number of syllables in it?

Pick a Number

 What do I need?

Ten pieces of card (playing-card size). Write the number 1 on three cards, number 2 on four cards and number 3 on three cards. If your child does not recognise numbers, draw the appropriate number of dots on each card instead and you can count them together.

 How to play

Spread the cards out face down, in front of you both.

Take turns to turn over a card and clap the number, three claps if 3 is on the card, and so on. Then look round the room you are in and find something with the right number of syllables – 'carpet' for 2, 'photo-frame' for 3, and so on.

You will need to say and clap together until you find something with the right number. Say the word out loud and clap as you work out the syllables.

Once you have found something with the right number, discard that card and take another from those left in front of you.

 Some more ideas

You can make this game easier by choosing three items in the room, one which is 1 syllable, one which is 2 syllables and one which is 3 syllables. For example, 'soap (1), flannel (2), shower gel (3)'. Say the items with your child. Then play as above. If you reduce the choices, your child can focus their attention on choosing the right number of syllables and not be distracted by other things in the room.

Another way to simplify the game is to start with cards with 1 or 2 on, so you are looking for words with one or two syllables only.

Each time you play the game do so in a different room; that exposes your child to a variety of words to practise with.

Post Boxes

⭐ What do I need?

Three post boxes. These may be home-made from shoe boxes, with a slit cut in the side; or you may have a post box from another game (such a shape sorter or money game). Pictures of varying syllable length (some are provided on p. 95, and the syllable lists on pages 89–90 give more ideas), paper and pen.

⭐ How to play

Draw 1, 2 and 3 on three separate pieces of paper (sticky paper if available) and attach one to the front of each post box. This determines which picture goes in which post box. The one-syllable words go in the box with 1 stuck on the front, and so on.

Go through all the pictures with your child and name them together. Then, getting your child to close their eyes for a minute, hide the pictures round the room. Let your child find one at a time. When they do so, they must say the word and clap the syllable(s) in it. They then post it into the right post box. If the clapping is not quite accurate, clap it with them or encourage them to listen to you saying and clapping the word. This is not a test. The right picture should always end up in the right box because you will have worked it out together.

When all the pictures have been found and posted, open the boxes and say and clap the little pile of pictures in each one. This helps to emphasise the syllables, as those in each box will all be the same.

⭐ Some more ideas

If your child is happy to let you join in, take turns to hide the pictures and find them. You may choose to make some deliberate mistakes when identifying the number of syllables and ask them for help.

If your post boxes are big enough, you could post toys or other real objects from round the house, or even treasures from a walk or visit to the park. Don't forget to identify the syllables first, and always say the word as you clap.

Syllable Lotto

 What do I need?

Lotto template photocopied (p. 92), nine counters or coins

 How to play

This is a game for your child to listen to and work out the number of syllables in words. You need to write 1 in three boxes on the lotto template, 2 in three boxes and 3 in three boxes. The numbers may be randomly distributed on the board.

You say a word, then your child must say it and clap out the number of syllables. Once they have worked it out, they may cover up one of the appropriate numbers on the board.

Continue to play until all the squares are covered up.

 Some more ideas

You may reverse roles with this game, and let your child say words for you to identify the number of syllables in.

You may also ring the changes by choosing a category of words to say and work out the number of syllables – for example, family names, football teams, towns and cities, fruit, animals, colours.

Washing Basket Rap

 What do I need?

Your basket of clean washing

 How to play

As your children help you with the job of sorting out the washing ready for putting it away, you can turn this into a time to play with syllables.

You are going to stamp the syllables and say the words at the same time.

Here are some examples:

- Zac's-T-shirt
- Mu-mmy's-jum-per
- Dad's-jeans
- Sa-rah's-blue-socks

 Some more ideas

Once your child has got the idea, you can make this funnier by stamping and saying the items really fast, or having lots of items to say together. For example:

Sa-mmy's-sock-and-jeans-and-top-and-shorts-and track-suit.

Animal Alliteration

 What do I need?

Selection of toy animals

 How to play

While you are playing together with toy animals, introduce the idea of the animals doing something that starts with the same sound as their name. For example:

- lion leaps
- sheep shivers
- mouse moans
- horse hurries.

 Some more ideas

You can continue this theme by describing the animal in a similar way. For example:

- cuddly cat
- mini-mouse
- funny frog
- terrible tiger.

Bath-time Fun

 What do I need?

Foam letters

 How to play

First stick some of the letters to the side of the bath.

Your child has to listen to a word you say and decide which letter it starts with. They then knock that letter into the bath. Continue until all the letters are in the bath water.

⭐ **Some more ideas**

You can reverse the roles in this game so your child has to say a word, and you knock the right letter into the water. Without knowing it, your child is then involved in thinking of words according to their sounds and in making judgements about whether you make the right choice of letter or not.

Book Worms

 What do I need?

Picture books and a puppet (or small cuddly toy)

 How to play

Choose a big book with plenty of busy pictures. Introduce your puppet who loves looking for pictures that start with one particular sound, such as *t*. Let the puppet have a look at the pictures in the book. Ask your child to help him find all the pictures that start with *t*. The child can keep a tally of how many pictures they find.

On a different day choose a different sound.

 Some more ideas

Let your child decide which sound/letter they want to hunt for.

You could suggest a picture which starts with the appropriate sound that you say you think might be in the book, and see if your child can find it.

Feely Bag

 What do I need?

Feely bag, selection of toys and things from round the house to fit in bag – an equal number all beginning with the same sound to the number beginning with a variety of other sounds.

Here are some ideas:

- boat, banana, bead, bag, book
- cup, comb, cat, cap, key
- sock, spoon, snake
- feather, frog, fish, phone.

 How to play

Introduce the feely bag. Explain that it has in it a jumble of toys and things and that you want to sort out those beginning with your target sound – let's say *b* – and all the rest that don't start with *b*. Take turns with your child to put your hand into the bag. Pull one toy out. Say what it is and work out what sound it starts with. Decide whether it goes in the pile of things starting with *b* or not.

When the bag is empty you should have a pile of things beginning with *b* and a pile of things that don't. Name the *b* things together, and then see if you can both think of some more words that start with the same sound.

 Some more ideas

If your child finds it hard to work out the first sound of the word, here are some strategies to help:

- Exaggerate the first sound of the word.
- Give a choice (also known as a 'forced alternative') – 'Does it start with *b* or *s*?'
- When selecting your toys, you could select things that start with contrasting sounds. For example, *b* is a short sound so you could contrast it with toys starting with long sounds, such as *s*, *f*, *sh*, *m*, *l*.

Finger Spelling

 What do I need?

Paper and pencils

 How to play

Ask your child to draw round one of their hands, with their fingers spread out. Give your child a letter to write in the palm of the hand on the paper (e.g. *f*). They then have to think of and write or draw five things beginning with that sound, one to go in each finger.

You can help by encouraging them to look round the room they are in, or giving them clues.

Some more ideas

Get the child to cut out their hands with the letter and words on and start a display of words and sounds. Each time you play with a different sound, you can add it to the display. The hand shapes could make a sound tree, or be added to the tops of stalks to make flowers.

Fun at Meal-time

★ What do I need?

Nothing, apart from your meal in front of you

★ How to play

This is the sort of game that demonstrates how you can play with sounds in words wherever you are and whatever you are doing. The idea is to identify the first sound for each of the items on your plate.

You can play this as an 'I spy with my little eye' game. If your meal were sausages, carrots, mash and gravy, you might then start with 'I spy with my little eye something beginning with *m*.'

You can extend this to trying to think of other food that starts with the same sound as what is on your plate. You can have lots of fun creating interesting food combinations. Would you add melon to your plate of sausages? Perhaps mushrooms would be better?

★ Some more ideas

Make sure that your child gets a go at choosing the sound you are looking for on your plates. If necessary give them some alternatives when it comes to thinking of other things that start with the same sound – for example, 'Does melon or peas start with the *m* like mash?'

I'm Thinking of ...

 What do I need?

Pictures (or real things) for miming

 How to play

Spread the pictures out in front of you both. Explain that this is a guessing game: your child is to guess what you are thinking about. You are going to give some clues to help. Begin by saying what sound the word starts with and then do a mime about the word.

Here are some examples:

- scissors   starts with *s*; mime cutting
- pencil   starts with *p*; mime drawing
- apple   starts with *a*; mime taking a bite.

 Some more ideas

This game is designed for your child to listen and work out the first sound of the word with the help that the mime gives. You can make it harder by taking turns to give the clues and guess.

Icing Biscuits

 What do I need?

Plain biscuits, small tubes of ready-made icing

 How to play

Most children like to do a bit of baking as long as they get to eat their creations. This provides for a phonics game at the same time.

You are going to ice letters on to the biscuits. Choose a letter and think of some things that start with that sound as you ice. As you choose different letters, see which one you can think of the most words for.

If you manage not to eat the biscuits before others in the family are home, test them by getting them to think of some words before they are allowed to choose one to eat.

 Some more ideas

You might choose to ice letters that represent the first sound of family members' names, so that they know which one is for them. Make sure you let your child do the working out. You might ask questions like these:

'Whom shall we make one for now?'
'What sound does their name start with?'
'Do you know what that letter looks like?'
'Shall I draw it so you can copy it?'

Let's go Shopping

⭐ **What do I need?**

Pencils and paper or card, pretend money

⭐ **How to play**

Explain to your child that you are going to set up a shop. It is a special shop. All the things in the shop have to start with the same sound. Choose a phoneme (e.g. *p*).

Ask the child to think of some things beginning with the sound and to draw them. You can get involved and help by drawing things your child suggests or making your own selection of words. (You may want to put in some pictures that do not start with the right sound to see if your child can tell you it was not right.)

When your child has a selection of pictures, you become the shopkeeper. You let them know whether each picture can go in your shop or not, according to whether it starts with the correct sound. Swap over and bring your pictures to the shop to see if they are acceptable.

Once the shop is fully stocked with items, the child can have fun going shopping and buying items that all start with the same sound. This is a great way to introduce new phonemes as it provides an activity rich in just one sound.

The following week change the phoneme and you have a newly stocked shop to play with.

⭐ **Some more ideas**

To make this harder, you may encourage your child to be creative with their pictures and think about the letter at the start of a phrase. For example, if the letter is *s*, a smiley face would be acceptable, as would a silly car.

Running to Sound

 What do I need?

Paper and pen, optional scooter or ride-on car

 How to play

Choose two letters which your child is going to listen out for at the beginning of words.

Here are some ideas:

- easy: b/s, f/g, m/t, p/c, l/p
- hard: p/b, t/d, m/n, l/w, c/g, s/f

Write one letter on one piece of paper and one on another. Place the papers either at opposite ends of the room or at a distance outside. Make sure your child knows what the letters are.

Now you are ready to play the game. You say a word which begins with one of the sounds and your child works out what sound is at the start of the word and runs, scoots or rides over to it. Encourage your child to say the word and the letter and then return to the middle of the space ready to listen to the next word you will say.

You can make variations by asking them sometimes to hop, jump, skip, walk, and so on to the correct letter.

 Some more ideas

Start off the game by saying only the sound on its own, not in a word: for example, *mmm* rather than 'moon'. Once your child is able to respond to the single sound said on its own, you can try putting it into simple short words: 'my', 'moo', 'me', and so on.

Most children like to be the boss, so you may like your child to tell you some words so that you have to run or scoot to the right sound. It can be good fun to get it wrong deliberately and run to the wrong letter. Can they tell you what was wrong?

Sounds Collage

 What do I need?

Old magazines, scissors, glue, paper

 How to play

Find a magazine for cutting up. Choose a sound (e.g. *m*). Together look through the magazine and find pictures of things beginning with that sound. Explain that the words may be describing words (adjectives) or doing words (verbs), not just names of things (nouns). Once they have found a picture, cut it out and create a sounds collage.

For a collage on *m*, you may have pictures of: monkey, money, man, Mummy, muddy boots, mirror, milk and mean face.

⭐ **Some more ideas**

It may help to have a look through the magazine yourself in advance so you find some that could be cut out and direct your child a little.

The collage can become a good talking point in the family. You can ask them, for instance, to guess why all those pictures were selected, or what they have in common.

Spin and Say

⭐ What do I need?

Some cards with categories written on. Suggested categories include: fruit, vegetable, boy's name, girl's name, country, place to visit, something you can wear, something in school, something associated with parties, animal, something you can hear, something that may be red, something you need a ticket for, a drink, a sport, something in a house, something at a zoo, something that needs cooking, name for a pet, television programme or film.

A spinner (see template on p. 93) with some letters on; suggested letters are: p, b, m, n, d, t, f, s, c, g, sh.

⭐ How to play

Have the category cards in a pile. Spin the spinner and say the letter that is chosen. Turn over a category card and get the child to think of a word in the category that starts with the phoneme. For example, if you spin *p* and turn over a category card for 'place to visit', they could answer Paris, Pizza Hut, park. If the answer is appropriate the child wins the card. Continue until all the cards have been won.

⭐ Some more ideas

Play with the whole family. Every member has to think of a word beginning with the chosen sound within the category that is turned over.

Think and Draw

 What do I need?

Paper, coloured pens

 How to play

This activity is about thinking of words beginning with a certain sound.

Agree on a sound and each write the letter for it on your piece of paper. Then both think of and draw some pictures beginning with that sound. The game is best if it is snappy, so allow about 1–2 minutes for this. You can make the game more fun by adding an element of competition – you get a point for a drawing only if no one else thought of it as well. That will encourage your child to think of words that are a little out of the ordinary. For example, given the sound *k*, many children would think of cat, king, cup and cake. More thought may mean they come up with cuddle, caterpillar, and so on.

Continue the game for as long as you like, changing the sound each time and adding up the scores as you go along.

 Some more ideas

Encourage your child to look round the room for things beginning with the sound if they get stuck, or to think of the names of people whom they could draw.

What's in this Room?

 What do I need?

Nothing

 How to play

Decide on a letter. The activity is to find something beginning with that letter in each room of the house. This will help to demonstrate that sounds and letters are all around us, not just to do with writing and paper.

You might choose to start with the letter sound that your child's name starts with. If that is *s*, for example, look round for things such as sock, soap, scissors and salt, or if it is *r*, you might find things such as rubber, roses, ring and rug.

 Some more ideas

You may like to use little sticky dots, which you put on the things you find in each room that start with your chosen sound.

You could create a little competition by seeing which room has the most things starting with a particular sound.

Cross it off

 What do I need?

Pen, paper

 How to play

Give your child a pen and paper. Ask them to write down the following consonants:

- p, b, t, d, ck, g, l, m, n, s, sh, f, th, z

or write them out before you start. Spread the letters out over the paper.

The aim of the game is for them to listen to a word that you will say and work out what the last sound in that word is. They then find the letter for the sound and cross it out. So, if you say 'goat', the child isolates the final sound as being *t*, and finds the letter *t* and crosses it out.

Encourage the child to say the word out loud and work out the final sound by trying to break the word up into the consonant vowel (first bit) and the last consonant; for example, re-d (red), na-me (name).

You can take this opportunity to use words that are not nouns because you don't need pictures for the game – for example, 'shine' (final sound *n*), 'hot' (final sound *t*). Continue until all the letters have been crossed out.

 Some more ideas

The game is easier if you restrict the number of sounds the child is listening for. You may start with four letters, but have each one written two or three times on the paper so that there are several opportunities to hear the sound in different words.

The child will probably enjoy thinking of words so that you can identify the last sound and have to cross letters off too.

Tiddlywinks

 What do I need?

Tiddlywinks counters, card with target board drawn on it (see p. 94)

 How to play

At the start of this game, select some sounds which are common at the ends of words and write them on the target board, one in each space. Suggested sounds are: *m, sh, f, t, k, s, d, g, n.*

You say a simple word with one of those sounds at the end, and your child identifies which sound they heard. This then becomes their target. They win a point if they can get their tiddlywinks on to the area where that letter is on the target board.

Keep going until all the letters have been accounted for.

 Some more ideas

Can your child think of words with those sounds at the end? If they can, play this game by taking turns to say a word, selecting the letter and trying to get your tiddlywinks into the right area.

You can also add a little competition. After your child has identified the correct letter, you both try to get your tiddlywink on the letter. Who gets it there first?

Where's the Spinner?

 What do I need?

A spinner (see template, p. 93) with some letters on – suggested letters are: *p, b, m, n, d, t, f, s, c, g, sh*

 How to play

Spin the spinner and say the letter that is chosen.

Your child then looks round the room they are in and finds something that has that sound at the end of the word.

For example, if a *d* is spun they find a picture of a bird on a poster.

Move to another room and spin again.

Go into every room of the house, including the garage, bathroom, and so on, and have some fun finding words.

⭐ **Some more ideas**

Your child may well need some help to find a word with the correct sound at the end of it. You might need to give some clues, direct their looking or give them a choice; for example, you spin an *m* and say to the child, 'Could it be a comb or a brush?'

Word Mime

 What do I need?

Things round the house

 How to play

Get together a collection of things from round the house. You need to think about the sound at the end of each word as this game relies on your child being able to identify the sound at the end of the various items. Explain that you are going to mime an item and they must guess what it is. Give them a sound clue first, such as 'It ends with sh', and mime a fish.

Take turns to do the mime and give the sound clue, and to work out what the item is. Continue until all the items have been mimed.

 Some more ideas

Naming the items before you start the game and identifying the last sounds will help the child once the game gets underway.

If you have a pencil handy, it may also help to write down the last sound of the item you are miming.

Guess my Picture

 What do I need?

Paper, pens, chalks, paints

 How to play

Think of something you can draw. Give your child a rhyming clue for the picture you are about to draw. For example, you say 'It rhymes with bee.' Then you start to draw a tree. See if they can guess what it is before you have finished the drawing.

Award points for words that rhyme, even if they are not correct, and award a further point for the correct word.

 Some more ideas

Keep saying the rhyming clue out loud with your child while you are drawing, and encourage them to think of some other rhyming words, nonsense words and real ones. This will help to guide them to the word you are thinking of.

You can have great creative fun by chalking on paths, doing big paintings on old wallpaper, and so on.

Model Animals

 What do I need?

Playdough or pencils and paper

 How to play

The aim of this game is to make up some rhyming pairs for animals while having fun with playdough (or pencils and paper if you prefer).

Identify some single-syllable animals – for example, dog, cat, mouse, fish, rat, horse, snake, bird, slug, frog, cow, pig, hen, ant.
Select an animal (e.g. snake) and think of some words that rhyme with it (e.g. cake, fake, lake, bake).

Let your child choose one of the rhyming words and then have fun trying to create it out of playdough (e.g. cake – snake).
The idea is that the model is of the animal, but also captures some of the features of the rhyming word. For example, a log frog might have branches instead of legs and leaves on its head.

Have lots of fun making rhyming creations.

 Some more ideas

Encourage lots of rhyming chatter while you are making up animals.

Leave your models out and encourage other family members or visiting friends to work out what the rhyming pair is.

You could take pictures of the models and email them to friends for their guesses. Let them know that they must be rhyming names.

Monster Names

 What do I need?

Paper and coloured pencils or paints, or junk modelling

 How to play

This activity demonstrates how you can bring fun sounds to practically any hobby or pastime. Ask your child to draw or make a funny-looking monster, the more peculiar the better, with the equipment you have chosen. You make one as well. When it is finished the creation will need a name. The catch is that the name must rhyme. Examples are: funky-wunky, lubby-hubby, sloppy-poppy. The child will have lots of fun making up the silly rhymes and deciding which one best suits their picture.

 Some more ideas

Give them some starts for the monster name, and let them finish the name off. For example:

- fussy-
- rippy-

See if they can make up a name with three rhymes in it (e.g. fuddy-suddy-duddy).

Nursery Rhyme Time

 What do I need?

Nothing, or book of nursery rhymes

 How to play

Ask your child to think of a nursery rhyme (or select one in the book). Say the rhyme together. Then say it again slowly and listen for the rhyming words.

Say 'I wonder which words are going to rhyme next?'

Encourage the child to think ahead and tell you the rhyming pairs. You can write down the rhyming pairs. It may be fun to discover which nursery rhyme has the most rhyming pairs.

 Some more ideas

Download the nursery rhyme from the internet or write it down. Read it through. Ask the child to underline the words that rhyme, and keep on saying the rhyming pairs to emphasise the concept of rhyme.

Having found the rhyming words in the nursery rhyme, see if they can change some of the words so that they still rhyme and still make sense. For example:

> Jack and Bill
> Went up the hill
> To fetch a pail of water.
> Jack fell down
> It made him brown
> And Bill went to tell his daughter.

Playdough

 What do I need?

Playdough or salt dough

 How to play

Think of a word that has some good rhymes. Select one of those words, and together see if, using playdough, you can make something that rhymes with the word you said.

For example, you say the word 'chair'. You might choose to make a pear or a bear to rhyme with it.

Here are some ideas for rhyming words:

- chair, mat, wish, house, socks, fun, sea.

⭐ **Some more ideas**

See how many things you can make that rhyme with just one word and keep a record of the number. Each time you play the game, choose another word and see how many things you can make that rhyme with it. Over time you can see which one has the most rhyming words to go with it.

Rhyming Consequences

 What do I need?

Pen, paper

 How to play

At the top of the piece of paper you write a simple word (e.g. hen).
You then fold the paper over to cover the word, and write a word that
rhymes with 'hen' underneath the fold. Fold this over so that your word
cannot be seen and hand the paper to your child. The child writes a
word that rhymes with 'hen'. (You do not know what each other has
written.) The paper is returned and you write another rhyming word
for 'hen'. This continues until the paper has been folded many times
and there are lots of words rhyming with 'hen' written on it.

When the paper is full, you can open it out and read all the rhyming
words. You will find it fun to see how many different words you
thought of.

Encourage your child to try different sound combinations and words
out loud as this helps their phonic skills.

 Some more ideas

Take turns to think of the first word to start off another rhyming word
(e.g. chain).

Rhyming Hide and Seek

 What do I need?

Pairs of pictures that rhyme. Some photocopiable pictures are provided to start you off (see p. 96).

 How to play

Name all the pictures. Ask your child to close their eyes as you hide all the pictures round your home or garden. As they go round and find them, ask them to name the pictures. Once they are all found, work together to match up the rhyming pairs. Say the pictures together and listen for the similarities. You may like to try to think of some other words that rhyme with those that you have found.

 Some more ideas

You can extend this game by taking turns to go and find matching pairs of rhyming pictures. You return only when you have found a pair, leaving the other cards in place ready for the next person.

You can also change the game by drawing or printing out some other rhyming pairs of pictures.

Travelling time

✪ **Syllable games**

Clapping Cars

How Long is that?

In the Jungle

Robot Talk

Ten Names

✪ **First sound games**

Finger Count

Finish it off

I went Shopping

Location, Location

Number Plates

Silly me

✪ **Last sound games**

Thumbs up

What's Missing?

What's my Word?

✪ **Rhyming games**

Rhyme Time

Rhyming Names

Who am I?

Clapping Cars

 What do I need?

Nothing

 How to play

Lots of children like looking at the different cars they see while on a journey. This game takes that interest and turns it into a useful syllable game.

You simply name the make or model of a car you see and clap the number of syllables that it has. Always say the word and clap it at the same time (although only if you are a passenger).

Here are some examples:

- As-tra
- Cit-roen-Pic-ass-o
- Hon-da-Ci-vic
- Land-Ro-ver

 Some more ideas

How many cars can you find with only one syllable in their name?

What is the car name with the most syllables that you can find?

How Long is that?

⭐ **What do I need?**

Nothing

⭐ **How to play**

This is another game about identifying the number of syllables that are in people's names. The idea is to find the longest name among those whom you know. As you say the name, count the syllables by clapping or tapping them out. You are allowed to include middle and surnames. Make this a contest by asking, 'Who can think of the longest name?' and joining in.

Always encourage your child to clap and say the word at the same time.

⭐ **Some more ideas**

If your child is struggling to think of names, you can give them some clues about people.

Once you have exhausted family and friends' names, why not move on to famous people?

In the Jungle

 What do I need?

Nothing

 How to play

Choose a special location (e.g. in the jungle). Together think of five or ten things (one for each finger) in that place. As you say the words, clap the syllables.

Always encourage your child to clap and say the word at the same time.

Examples might include:

> monkey, tiger, elephant, vines, bats, parrots, fruit

Make the places you choose exciting, and try to think about things you would really like to see, or eat or smell.

For example:

- Chinese restaurant
- Farm
- Australia
- Grandma's house.

 Some more ideas

If your child is struggling to think of things, you can give them some clues.

Try to give clues for words with several syllables, so that your child gets practice and experience of words of differing lengths.

Robot Talk

 What do I need?

Nothing

 How to play

This activity gives practise in breaking words into syllables. Robot talk is characterised by speaking one syllable at a time, in a monotone voice. Your child will have lots of fun talking like a robot.

You will need to demonstrate the talking to start with. Using robot talk yourself, ask your child to say their name like a robot. For example:

> What-is-your-name?
> My-name-is-Darr-en.

Then play a game while looking out of the car window. Take turns to look out and say what you can see in robot talk, like this:

> I-can-see-a-trac-tor.
> I-can-see-a-fire-en-gine.
> I-can-see-some-hor-ses.

 Some more ideas

Keep the sentences short and encourage some physical movement with each syllable – for example, jerky hand movements (as a robot might make) or clapping.

You might try taking turns to interview your robot, using questions such as these:

> Where do you live?
> What do you eat?
> What is your planet like?

Ten Names

 What do I need?

Nothing

 How to play

This game is about identifying the number of syllables that are in people's names.

Start with one-syllable names. Ask your child to think of ten names with only one syllable. They can keep a tally on their fingers.

For example:

> Tom, Raj, Jess, Deb, Mike, Eve.

Always encourage the child to clap and say the word at the same time. You can join in by tapping or nodding to mark the syllables.

Once this has been achieved, do the same for two- and three-syllable names.

 Some more ideas

Don't limit the game to ten. Ask how many names with one syllable they can think of in five minutes. If your child is struggling to think of names, give them some clues.

For example:

> Think of your cousins.
> Who is Halina's sister?

Finger Count

 What do I need?

Nothing

 How to play

This is a simple game, useful for filling in a few minutes on a car journey. Give your child a sound (e.g. *s*) and ask them to think of ten words beginning with that sound as fast as they can, counting on their fingers.

Don't forget that the words do not have to be nouns (naming words), but may be adjectives, verbs, and so on.

The selection of words for *s* might include:

- some, sunny, school, six, sorry, singing, soapy, sad, silly.

 Some more ideas

You might like to take turns to think of words. This will help if your child is finding it difficult to think of words as you can prompt them with your choices. For example, your suggesting 'six' might prompt them to say 'seven'.

Finish it off

 What do I need?

Nothing

 How to play

You make up the start of an alliterative sentence (in which most of the words start with the same sound) and ask your child to think of lots of different ways of finishing it off. For example:

- Sally smiled sweetly at … Sarah / sausages / the sweets
- Naughty Nicky … nibbled nuts / knew nothing / never told the truth
- Rabbits running … round and round / round the red robin
- Cuddly Koala ... kisses Carly / colours cars / coughs.

 Some more ideas

You may find you need to give your child some prompts or clues to think of an appropriate word.

If they like doing this game, maybe you could see how long you can keep the sentence going, asking them to predict how many words starting with the same sound there will be.

I went Shopping

 What do I need?

Nothing

 How to play

Start the game by deciding on a sound, let's say *p*. You say 'I went to Tesco and I bought some pencils.' Ask your child to think of something else that starts with the same sound. For example:

> I went to Tesco and I bought some pencils and a pizza.

How many items can you generate and remember?

Choose a different sound. Find out which sound generates the most items.

 Some more ideas

It will help your child if you give clues for possible items; for example, 'I can think of something that you can eat, and you can mash them or make them into chips' for 'potato'.

Location, Location

 What do I need?

Nothing

 How to play

Choose a location. It could be the place where you are going, where you have just been, or a place you pass on your journey. Your task, with your child, is to think of something beginning with each letter of the alphabet that you find in that place. For example, if the location is 'leisure centre':

- a for athlete
- b for ball
- c for class
- d for door
- e for exercise.

And for 'Grandma's house':

- a for apple pie
- b for bed
- c for cat
- d for dominoes.

 Some more ideas

You may find you need to give some clues for words; for example, 'It starts with *t* and it is what Granny puts her plate on at lunchtime' for 'table'.

Number Plates

 What do I need?

Nothing

 How to play

Choose the number plate of a car you are following. Identify the letters on the number plate and decide on a mini-shopping list of things that start with the letters on the number plate. For example, for YH53 OMP your list could be:

> yogurt, hairbrush, orange, mushy peas, pizza.

 Some more ideas

You may want to make this harder by having all the items in one category (e.g. fruit and vegetables, household items, things you can buy from Argos or a garden centre).

Silly me

 What do I need?

Nothing

 How to play

This is a listening game. Point out some things you see as you are travelling (e.g. police car, horse, moon, bike). This becomes a listening game when you say some of the words incorrectly by substituting a different sound for the first sound of the word. Taking the examples above, you might say:

- 'molice car' for police car
- 'borse' for horse
- 'soon' for moon
- 'pike' for bike.

Can your child tell you if you said it the right way or not? Ask if all the sounds were correct for the word. If they point out a mistake, say, 'Silly me! What was wrong? What should I have said?'

If necessary encourage the child to identify the initial sound and tell you what it is (e.g. 'molice car'). Can they tell you that it should not be *m* and should be *p* at the beginning of the word?

 Some more ideas

Your child will probably love to say some words the wrong way for you. This is good fun. You can push them a little by failing to identify the wrong sound and asking them for some help. In this way they become the teacher and the learner at the same time.

Thumbs up

 What do I need?

Nothing

 How to play

This quick and easy game concentrates on listening for sounds at the ends of words. You say, for example, '"Sock" ends with *k*', and your child must indicate if you are right with thumbs up or thumbs down.

Children love doing the thumbs up and down signals.

Other examples:

- 'crane' ends with n
- 'bird' ends with g
- 'school' ends with s
- 'shop' ends with b.

 Some more ideas

Give the child the option of putting out their thumbs horizontally to mean 'I'm not sure.' Then you can help them work it out.

Encourage your child to say the word out loud as it gives them the chance to hear the sounds again.

What's Missing?

 What do I need?

Nothing

 How to play

This is a listening game. Look round and say something you can see. Say it with the last sound of the word missing. Can your child say the word the right way, and tell you the sound that was missing? For example:

You might say *bu* for 'bus'. Can the child tell you that it is an *s* that is missing from the end?

 Some more ideas

You can make this easier to start with by simply asking the child whether you said the word correctly or not. You can then ask, 'I wonder if you can tell me what the sound at the end should be.' Slightly exaggerate the last sound to help them hear it: '"Busss, busss.". What sound can you hear at the end of the word?'

If your child focuses on other sounds, accept those and then refocus on the missing sound, like this:

'Yes, there is a *b* sound. I can hear *b* at the beginning of the word. What else can you hear? "Bus".'

What's my Word?

 What do I need?

Nothing

 How to play

This is a quick game to play for just a few minutes. It is a great way to practise thinking of sounds at the end of words.

Start the game by saying 'I'm thinking of a word and it starts like this …'. An example is *ma*. Your child then suggests sounds that could finish the word. In this instance possible sounds include *t* for 'mat', *p* for 'map', *n* for 'man' and *ch* for 'match'.

Encourage your child to speak out loud as they try out different sounds at the end of your word. When they think they have a real word then they can ask if that is the word you are thinking of.

Only accept real words. If a child suggests a non English word, but the blending was correct – for example, 'mab', you can praise the blending and ask them whether they think that is a real word.

 Some more ideas

In addition to saying how your word starts, you could give a clue about the meaning. For example, your word is 'hat' so you say that you are thinking of a word starting with *ha* and it is something you put on your head.

Ask your child what the sound is that goes on the end of the word to make it sound right; answer in this case, 't'.

Rhyme Time

 What do I need?

Nothing

 How to play

You are going to make up some silly rhymes about animals.
You start. For example:

- I am a fish and I live in a dish.
- I am a bunny and I am funny.

Ask your child to think of an animal and make up a rhyme. If their attempt does not rhyme, help them out by thinking of some words that rhyme with their animal. The child can then choose which word they want to try to use in their silly sentence.

 Some more ideas

Decide on the number of animals for which you will make up silly rhymes – perhaps ten. Once you have achieved this, change to another category and try making up rhyming sentences for that.

Categories might include: countries, food, TV characters.

Here are some examples:

- I dance in France.
- The rain in Spain is a pain.
- My bread is under my bed.
- I like jam and ham.
- Dr Who is on the loo.
- Harry Potter is getting hotter.

Rhyming Names

 What do I need?

Nothing

 How to play

Explain that you are going to make rhymes with everyone's name, for example:

- Lin has a tin.
- Mac likes to quack
- Eva found a lever.
- Kyle runs a mile.

Ask the child to generate a rhyme for their name. Select one name from among your family and see if they can think of a rhyming description. If no ideas are forthcoming, or the descriptions do not rhyme, you will need to start prompting a rhyme, for example:

> Mary. Well, let's make some rhyming words. Some of them will be silly words and some of them will be real. Let's have a go. Parey, fairy, hairy, dairy, scary …

It is important that the child understands the concept that rhyming words may not be spelt the same way, and that words can rhyme even if they are not real English words.

⭐ **Some more ideas**

When you get home the child may like to draw one or two of their favourite rhymes. For example: 'Mary likes to be scary.'

If your child is struggling to generate rhymes, you can take this game back to a rhyme detection task. You choose a name and start saying words, of which some rhyme and some don't. Can they tell you which ones rhyme? Can they say the rhyming pair? For example, ask if these rhyme or not:

- Miles/moles
- Miles/tiles
- Miles/mill.

Who am I?

 What do I need?

Nothing

 How to play

This is a listening game in which you give clues and your child has to use the information you give and guess what you are thinking of.

Your clues must give some information about what your word rhymes with, as well as something about its meaning. For example:

- I rhyme with dog and I love to croak. (Frog)
- I rhyme with pose and I am nice to smell. (Rose)
- I rhyme with rain and I fly in the sky. (Plane)

Ask the child to guess what you are thinking of from the riddle you have given them.

⭐ **Some more ideas**

Make sure that your child takes note of the rhyming part of the clue. When they make their guess ask them to say it as well as your rhyming word. In the examples above this would be 'dog/frog', 'pose/rose' and 'rain/plane'.

Your child might like to try making some clues for you to guess. Make sure they include a rhyming clue. (This will be quite hard, so give them time to come up with their clues.)

Out and about

✪ **Syllable games**

Jumping Jacks

Parked Cars

Striding out

Supermarket Syllables

✪ **First sound games**

Catch and Say

I Hear with my Little Ear

Interesting Treasure

Lamp Posts

Muddy Marks

Scavenger Hunt

Time to Vote

✪ **Last sound games**

Change the Sound

Final Run

Run like a Monkey

✪ **Rhyming games**

Drawing in the Sand

I Spy

Poems in the Sand

Rhyming Hoops

Jumping Jacks

 What do I need?

Four big hoops or string to make circles with, or chalks to draw circles in a line

 How to play

Lay (or draw) the hoops in a line so that your child can jump from one to another. The aim is to jump through one hoop as they say one syllable of a word; for example:

- Ra-chel (2 jumps)
- Ta-li-a (3 jumps)
- Jack (1 jump).

It is a good idea for you to do this first to show the child what to do. You may also help them by getting them to say their name broken down into syllables before they jump into the hoops. Then ask them to jump and say their name at the same time.

When they have finished jumping and saying their name, count the number of hoops jumped through with them and ask them to confirm how many syllables there are in their name.

Take turns to jump through the hoops saying the names of friends and family. Who has the longest name?

⭐ **Some more ideas**

If the child is struggling to break words down into syllables, you jump through the hoops and say the name together with your child.

You can make the game a little harder by jumping and saying the full names of people (e.g. Ry-an-Mart-in-Long-fell-ow).

Parked Cars

 What do I need?

Access to lines of parked cars

 How to play

The aim of this game is to have fun while marking out syllables in words.

Say a word and together with your child work out how many syllables there are in it. Then run past the right number of parked cars as you say the syllables in the word.

For example, you might choose the word 'computer'. Say *com* as you run past the first car, *pu* as you run past the second and *ter* as you run past the third.

⭐ **Some more ideas**

If you are feeing particularly energetic, you can run and break up into syllables whole phrases or sentences. For example:

- I-can-run-fast-er-than-Ell-ie.
- I-like-jump-ing.

Striding out

 What do I need?

Nothing

 How to play

The aim of this walking game is to have fun while marking out syllables in words.

Look round the area you are walking/playing in. Choose something and say the word(s). Together with your child work out how many syllables there are in it. Then stride out the number of syllables there are in the word(s), saying the word(s) at the same time.

Here are some examples:

- round-a-bout
- mu-ddy-pu-ddle
- sti-cky-buds.

 Some more ideas

You can make this more fun by thinking about your strides. You might be giants with huge strides, or little creatures with tiny little steps. You could be kangaroos and boing your way round as you mark out the syllables.

Remember always say the word as you make your steps.

Supermarket Syllables

 What do I need?

Nothing

 How to play

As you go round the supermarket, take the opportunity to clap out some syllables. Spend a couple of extra minutes in the fruit and vegetable department and name and clap some of the things your child points out. Here are some examples:

- ki-wi-fruit
- ba-na-na
- pot-a-to
- caul-i-flow-er.

Always say the word and clap it together.

 Some more ideas

Ask the child to find the item with the longest number of syllables. Ask how many things they can see with two syllables. Look out for items with three syllables.

Catch and Say

 What do I need?

Ball or beanbag

 How to play

You can play this game with just two of you, but friends or brothers and sisters joining in will make it more fun. Stand facing each other or in a circle. You choose an initial sound (e.g. *p*). As you throw the ball to each other you must say a word beginning with *p*. If someone cannot think of a word they sit down until there is only one person standing. That person chooses the next sound to play with.

Some more ideas

If someone cannot think of a word, give them some clues. For example, 'I can think of an animal in a farm and it has a curly tail.'

Remember that the words do not have to be nouns. They could be verbs (playing, pouring, peeping) or adjectives (pretty, poor, pink). You could use proper nouns (Peter, Parvin, Poppy, Portugal, Pizza Hut, Peppa Pig).

You may want to give the child a choice of words if they are finding it difficult to think of one themselves. For example, for *p* you might give one of the following options:

- Can we have parachute or milkshake?
- Which one starts with *p*: 'pour' or 'four'?

To make the game a little harder, establish a rhythm that puts a time pressure on the child to say a word (e.g. '1, 2, 3, pig').

I Hear with my Little Ear

 What do I need?

Nothing

 How to play

While you are walking or playing outside, this is a great game to encourage your child to listen to the sounds around them. It is a version of I Spy with my Little Eye. Stop and listen to the sounds you can hear. Then say, 'I hear with my little ear, something beginning with …' and give the first sound of what you have identified. Among the things you hear may be: plane, car, bee, birds, wind, sea, runners, train, children.

Encourage your child to listen, look round and say the words they are thinking of. This will develop the skill of isolating initial sounds in words.

If your child chooses a word that starts with a different sound, work out together what sound it does begin with, remind them of your sound and ask them to guess again.

 Some more ideas

You may like to start off by working out some of the things you can hear together. For example, 'I can hear a plane and a bike. What can you hear?'

Only after you have tuned your child into the sounds around you do you try to play the game.

If you think it useful, work out together the first sound of each thing you can hear before you start the game.

Interesting Treasure

 What do I need?

A small bag or container would be useful, but is not essential

 How to play

While you are enjoying being out and about, look out for some interesting treasure. The items you choose may include a beautiful pebble, an interestingly shaped piece of wood, a feather, a huge leaf and a shell.

At some point when you take a rest, spread your treasure out on the ground and work out together what sound each piece starts with. For example, 'feather' starts with *f*.

Write the letter next to each item in whatever way you can – in the sand or mud or using grass or twigs.

Ask if there are any items that share the same first sound.

 Some more ideas

Can you also work out together the last sound of each piece of treasure?

Are there any items that share the same last letter?

Lamp Posts

 What do I need?

Road with lamp posts

 How to play

This activity uses the lamp posts as the start and finish of each turn. As you walk decide on a sound. By the time you reach the next lamp post, you both need to have thought of a word beginning with that sound. Check that you agree with each other's choice and then decide on another letter. You could work your way through the alphabet, depending on how long your walk is!

 Some more ideas

You may want to focus on some letters or sounds that your child is having difficulty with, but make sure you also include some that are relatively easy so that it is not too much hard work.

You can make the game more demanding by having to think of lots of words (not just one) beginning with a specific sound while you are between two lamp posts.

You could make this harder by limiting the choice of words; for example, words starting with *b* which are things to eat, or words beginning with *c* that are people's names.

Muddy Marks

 What do I need?

Mud or sand, sticks and leaves. If you are playing this at home you could use beans or seeds on a tray.

 How to play

The fun of this game is the drawing – in mud or sand, or making the shape of a letter with beans or seeds. Agree on a letter and draw it in the mud. You then take turns to think of things that start with that sound. Alternatively you can take turns to think of a word that begins with a sound that the other person has to guess. When you have finished that letter rub it out and write down a different letter.

If you are using seeds or beans, your child makes the letter by arranging the seeds into the letter shape.

The combination of the physical movements and making the sounds is a useful aid to making the links between letters and sounds.

Some more ideas

Start by writing the first letter of each other's name. Can you each think of some other words that begin with the same sound?

Make the game one about other people's names. The letter you choose to write or make must be the first letter of the name of someone you know.

Scavenger Hunt

 What do I need?

To be outside, perhaps in a park or garden, or on the beach

 How to play

Send your child off to find something beginning with a sound that you will give them. For example, you might ask them to find something beginning with *p* and they return with a pebble, some paper or a petal.

You then give them another sound and continue for as long as you want.

 Some more ideas

You could give your child eight to ten letters written on a piece of paper. They have to find things beginning with each of those sounds. You could play this with family and friends as well; if you have teams the first team to return with an item for each sound is the winner.

Time to Vote

 What do I need?

Mud or sand, or sticks and leaves

 How to play

This is a listening and running game. Get your child to draw a big cross in the mud or sand (or create one with the sticks and leaves). Then ask them to run a few paces away and draw a tick in the mud. Tell them you are going to make a statement and they have to signal whether what you said is right or not. They run to the correct sign as drawn in the mud. Here are some examples:

- 'Caterpillar' starts with *p*.
- 'Sand' starts with an *s*.
- 'Butterfly' starts with *m*.

 Some more ideas

If the child is having problems with particular speech sounds or sometimes says the wrong sound when attempting to spell a word, this activity can be individualised for them. Take the sounds they regularly confuse and use them in this game. For example, if they regularly mix up the *sh* and *s* sounds, you could choose a group of words beginning with one of those sounds.

You could extend this game to make statements about syllables, sounds at the ends of words or rhymes. For example:

- 'Sandcastle' has 2 syllables.
- 'Ship' ends with the *p* sound.
- 'Spade' and 'fish' rhyme.

Change the Sound

 What do I need?

A small bag or container would be useful, but is not essential

 How to play

Find some bits and pieces such as a twig, leaf, nut, stone, shell or piece of seaweed. Put them in your bag if you are using one. Take them back to your base or take a break where you are, tip out your finds and play a funny game with the sounds of the words.

The point of the game is to have fun changing the sounds in the words and seeing if you can make other real words.

Here is an example:

- Twig: change the *g* and try *n* (twin), *d* (twid), *k* (twik).

If your child can substitute the sounds and say the made-up words, they are developing a useful phonic skill. You will probably need to give some examples before they can do this.

You will find yourself making a lot of words which are not real English words. This is fine as the skill being practised is to change the last sound.

Some more ideas

Rather than waiting until you have a bag full of items, you could do this as you go along. You may want to write the word down (in mud or sand if outside), then cross out the last letter and try writing in the new sound to read and say.

Final Run

 What do I need?

Twigs or mud, lots of leaves or stones (or something similar)

 How to play

Identify two places to run to – for instance, trees, bushes, gate posts. Choose two letters. These are the ones you will be listening for at the ends of words, so choose letters for which you can think of plenty of words. Using twigs or drawing in mud, write one letter near each place you have chosen.

Go back to the start. You say a word ending with one of the chosen sounds. Your child has to work out which letter the sound starts with and run to the appropriate place. Have a pile of leaves, stones or some other items ready; your child can take one of these items to the place. When all the items have been placed, the game is over.

 Some more ideas

You might need to draw attention to the last sound, like this: 'It's a ball. Ball. What sound can you hear at the end of that?'

If the game remains too hard, you can repeat the above and give a choice of last sounds: 'Does it end with *l* or *s*?'

 Suggested word list

Final g
bag, dog, egg, flag, frog, jug, leg, mug, peg, pig, plug, rug

Final c/k
bike, black, book, cake, clock, duck, fork, lake, neck, sock, stick

Final s
bus, rice, dress, face, glass, grass, horse, house, mouse, nurse, police

Final t
boat, carpet, carrot, cat, coat, mat, rat, dart, eight, feet, gate, hat, kite, net, nut, plate, root, yacht

Final m
arm, bomb, comb, cream, farm, jam, game, lamb, room, swim, thumb

Final p
cup, pipe, rope, sheep, soap, shop

Run like a Monkey

 What do I need?

Sticks and leaves

 How to play

Find some bits and pieces (twigs, leaves, seaweed, etc.) to create some letters with. Make four different letters and space them a good few paces apart. Your child has to run to the sound they hear at the end of the word you say. For example, if you make the letters *m, t, f, p,* you might say:

- 'Home' ... what sound can you hear at the end?
- 'Eight' ... what sound is at the end?

To make this more fun, ask them to move to the right letter in the way that various animals would (e.g. move like a snake, an elephant, a crocodile, a monkey).

 Some more ideas

You can make this easier by reducing the number of choices available, using only two letters at first. If your child finds hearing the sounds at the end hard, it will help if you get them to listen to words that are only a vowel–consonant combination. For example:

- eat, arm, up, odd, eight, am, it, ape.

These words don't need to be real ones for the purposes of this game. You can make some up as long as their last sound is one you have made ready for your child to run to – for example: 'oof', 'ite', 'arp'.

Drawing in the Sand

 What do I need?

Sand, either on the beach or in a sand pit. You could also do this in mud.

 How to play

With your child, draw some pictures of simple-sounding words in the sand.

The fun starts as you make up a rhyming word for one of the pictures drawn. Ask the child to find the picture that rhymes with the word you say and scrub that picture out.

Here are some examples for when you have drawn a house, tree, car, apple and teddy:

- You say 'free', and they find the picture of a tree and rub it out.
- You say 'heady' and they find the picture of a teddy.

Don't forget that you can make up words that rhyme with the pictures.

 Some more ideas

Take turns to make the rhyming word for each other to work out. As you rub out the picture, make some more words rhyming with the one you have said.

I Spy

 What do I need?

Nothing

 How to play

This is a simple twist on the classic game of I Spy with my Little Eye. Instead of giving your child the first sound of the object you have identified, you say, 'I spy with my little eye something that rhymes with ...'

If you have identified a tree, for example, you could say that it rhymes with 'see'.

 Some more ideas

If the child is struggling to find the object you have thought of, give some other clue to do with where it is or its meaning. For example, for 'tree', you might say:

'It is very tall, it is covered in leaves, and it rhymes with "see".'

Remember that it is fine to make up rhymes that are not real words.

Poems in the Sand

 What do I need?

Sand, either on the beach or in a sand pit

 How to play

Choose a simple word for which you can generate lots of rhyming words – for example, 'cat'. Ask your child to help you think of as many rhyming words as possible for your target word. Draw them in the sand together.

Work together to make up a poem with as many of those rhyming words in it as possible, for example:

> The cat on the mat
> Sat on a rat
> And got very fat.
> The rat had a bat
> To pat the fat cat
> Who sat all day on the mat.

When you have used all the words for things you have drawn, wipe the sand clean and start again with a different word.

 Some more ideas

You might prefer to start this game by making a sentence or phrase with two rhyming words in it, rather than a whole poem.

Rhyming Hoops

 What do I need?

Hoops or circles drawn in sand or mud

 How to play

Put down three hoops in a line. Explain that you are going to make rhymes, and that for each rhyming word they can say, they jump through a hoop. The target is to make three rhyming words and get to the end of the hoops. You show them by saying and jumping – for example, 'say, hay, may'.

Give your child a CVC (consonant– vowel– consonant) or CV (consonant–vowel) word. See below for some suggested words.

Children love to jump so you can play this over and over again.

 Some more ideas

If the child is finding it hard to make up rhyming words, try giving them a sound to make the rhyme with. For example:

- 'Car'; try *f* ... 'far'. Does that rhyme with 'car'?
  'Car' – 'far.'

You can also let the child jump through the hoops as you make rhyming words.

Once they can make three rhyming words, add more hoops or circles, up to five. Ask them if they can make five rhymes in all.

Remember that it is fine to make up rhymes that are not real words.

 Suggested words

tee	moo	car	four
high	go	pay	cat
leg	tap	man	ball
pick			

Word lists

Here is a table to help you think of words that start and finish with individual sounds. You will notice that they are listed in sound groups, not according to how they are spelt. The lists are not exhaustive, but are intended to give you some ideas to use when you are playing the games.

Letter sound	First sound		Last sound	
a	apple astronaut alphabet animals	alligator ant angry		
b	bag banana bed bug bear bird butterfly biscuit	bath bowl boat button baby balloon beach bat bottle	rub crab cub tub robe	
c and k	cake king key cup cushion cat kangaroo kite carrot	caterpillar curtain carpet car candle cow camera camel	bike clock shark book milk cook look sock bark	dark hook mike rake kick lick pack park pork tick

Letter sound	First sound		Last sound	
d	door	dinner	bed	made
	dinosaur	dig	bird	road
	digger	dancer	spade	mud
	dog	duck	lid	hood
	dark		food	lid
	doctor		shed	blade
			field	wood
				dad
e	egg	explore		
	elephant	empty		
	end			
f	fish	four	leaf	cough
	frog	five	knife	tough
	food	finger	roof	laugh
	fan	field	calf	rough
	fog	fairy	loaf	
	flower	face	half	
	firework	fast	hoof	
	fireman	feet	woof	
	fire		if	
g	goat	give	egg	big
	game	guitar	leg	dig
	gate	guess	pig	hug
	girl		mug	plug
	grass		log	fog
	go		frog	wig
	good		bag	
h	hair	heart		
	hat	hungry		
	hip	hot		
	ham	horse		
	hand	home		
	hamburger			

Sounds Fun!

Letter sound	First sound		Last sound	
i	itch	inside		
	igloo	invention		
j	jelly	jacket	hedge	sledge
	giraffe	juice	badge	fridge
	joke	jumping	edge	sledge
	jeans		fudge	
l	leg	light	ball	smile
	lolly	lamp	hall	well
	ladder	laugh	hill	crawl
	leaf	listen	hole	owl
	letter	left	roll	bowl
	lips	little	mole	jail
	lion	lizard	pill	sail
	lorry	lunch	girl	nail
	love		shell	wall
m	man	magic	ham	room
	map	make	comb	lime
	monster	medicine	time	same
	monkey	mouse	drum	foam
	moon	mud	cream	home
	mouth	milk	lamb	warm
	money	mum	plum	
	mirror		gum	
n	nose	noodles	moon	hen
	net	numbers	prawn	mean
	knife		spoon	man
	nine		ten	fin
	nest		nine	sun
	next		pine	bean
	night		line	run
o	orange	off		
	octopus	on		
	old	opposite		

Letter sound	First sound		Last sound	
p	pen	paper	up	rip
	potato	peel	cup	rap
	penguin	people	sheep	hip
	pink	paint	rope	sharp
	penny	pie	map	hoop
	pebble	pizza	leap	
	pan	police	dip	
	purse	pig	lip	
	pasta	popcorn	tap	
q	queen	quiz		
	question	quilt		
r	ring	ride		
	robin	rain		
	red	road		
	rubber	rainbow		
	river	rabbit		
	rock	rocket		
	rhino	room		
s	sun	sad	bus	kiss
	sink	sing	face	ice
	sofa	sister	mouse	lace
	sea	soap	horse	dice
	sand	summer	house	dress
	seven		grass	boss
	six		glass	rice
			purse	
t	ten	table	hot	shut
	two	teeth	tent	shout
	tent	toothpaste	pot	mat
	tools	tickle	bat	rat
	tractor	time	bite	right
	tiger	top	kite	seat
	talk	T-shirt	coat	foot
			cot	meat
			light	write

Sound Fun!

Letter sound	First sound		Last sound	
u	umbrella up	under uncle		
v	vase vacuum vegetables very		five brave have hive wave move	cave curve love serve live give
w	water witch wave white walk wish	wheels windy whistle window wood		
y	yes yogurt yacht yellow	yawn young yesterday		
z	zoo zip zebra	zigzag	fizz eyes nose	buzz news
sh	shoe sugar shell shower shut shy	shorts shapes sheep shark shout	fish wish wash flash posh	sash bash mesh flesh mush
ch	chicken chocolate chimney cheese chair	chick	catch match witch patch hatch	each peach pouch watch
th	thumb thistle thunder	thirsty thin throw		

Syllable lists

Here is a table of words with one, two and three syllables to help you when you are playing games with syllables. The list is not exhaustive; it is intended to get you started.

1 syllable	2 syllables	3 syllables
mug	table	computer
car	curtain	frying pan
sink	scissors	radio
chair	sofa	dishwasher
fridge	kitchen	tablemat
bed	towel	pyjamas
bath	shower	dressing gown
brush	toothpaste	rubber duck
door	window	letterbox
grass	ladder	climbing frame
bike	scooter	rugby ball
hoop	flower	bird feeder
kite	robin	lawn mower
dog	spider	elephant
mouse	lion	dinosaur
bird	peacock	ladybird
frog	giraffe	butterfly
milk	milkshake	marmalade
bread	coffee	margarine
grape	melon	banana

Sound Fun!

jam	butter	pineapple
crisps	carrot	broccoli
chips	cookie	Rice Krispies®
peas	pizza	sausages
brick	jigsaw	marble run
book	pencil	dressing up
glue	CD	roundabout

What to do if you are concerned about your child's development

If you are concerned about your child's speech and language development, you should talk to a health professional about it. Your health visitor or GP will be able to give you advice. You can refer yourself to the speech and language therapy service, and will normally be able to do this through your local health centre. Speech and language therapists assess your child and then advise whether therapy is necessary.

If your child is already at school, you may find it useful to talk to their class teacher or the school Special Needs Co-ordinator regarding your concerns. They will be able to tell you whether your child's difficulties are affecting their school work and their social development.

Useful websites

Information and advice sheets

talkingpoint.org.uk
ican.org.uk
afasicengland.org.uk

Sources for speech and language therapy

rcslt.org the Royal College of Speech and Language Therapists
helpwithtalking.com the Independent Speech and Language
    Association

Lotto template

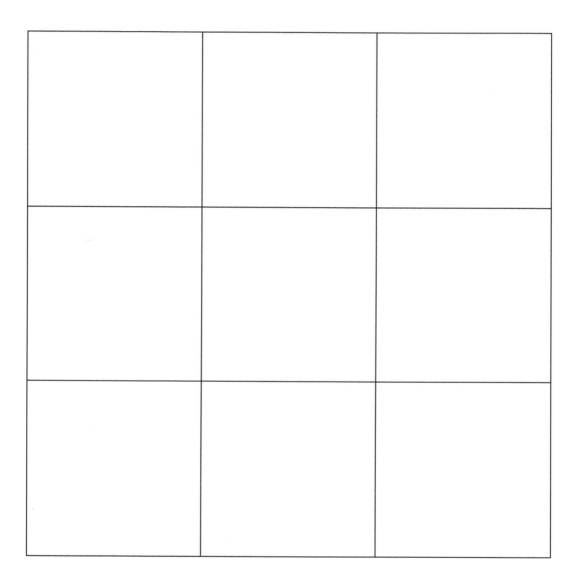

Spinner template

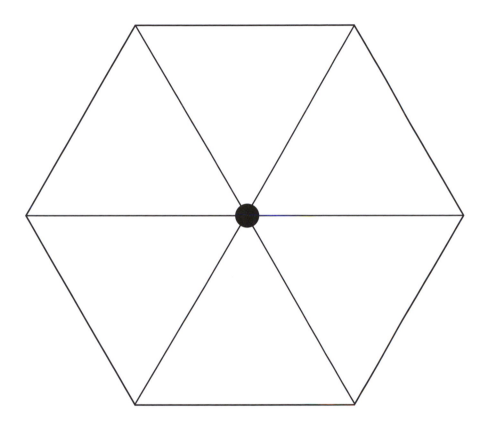

Tiddlywinks target card

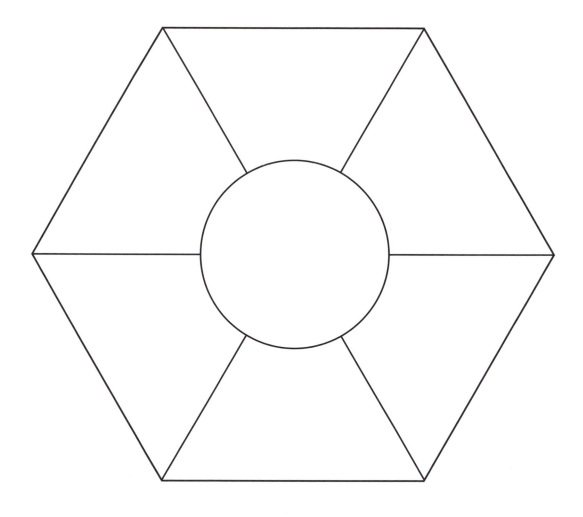

94

Pictures of things with 1, 2 or 3 syllables

Pictures of things that rhyme